For Oliver
with admiration —
Rennie

North Northeast

W
N
S

NORTH NORTHEAST

Rennie McQuilkin

Drawings by Sarah McQuilkin

1985

WILLIAM L. BAUHAN, PUBLISHER

DUBLIN, NEW HAMPSHIRE

LIBRARY OF CONGRESS CATALOGUING IN PUBLICATION DATA:

McQuilkin, Rennie, 1936-
North northeast.
1. New England—Poetry. I. Title.
PS3563.C65N6 1985 811'.54 85-13343
ISBN 0-87233-080-X
ISBN 0-87233-081-8 (pbk.)

Published 1985 by William L. Bauhan, Publisher
Old County Road, Dublin, New Hampshire, 03444.
Printed in the United States of America.

For Mouse

Acknowledgments

GRATEFUL acknowledgment is made to the Connecticut Commission on the Arts and to the National Endowment for the Arts, whose grants made possible the completion of this collection, and to the following publications for permission to reprint poems which first appeared in their pages.

ANTHOLOGY OF MAGAZINE VERSE AND YEARBOOK OF AMERICAN POETRY. *New England Greenhouse, Tree Man*

THE ANTIGONISH REVIEW. *The Burning Off*

APPLE: AN ANTHOLOGY OF UPSTATE NEW YORK POETRY. *Celebration*

THE BALL STATE UNIVERSITY FORUM. *Sickle Moon: A Little Lunacy, That Time*

BLUE UNICORN. *Storm System, The Inside Cat*

THE BRIGHTON-PITTSFORD POST. *Squirrel*

THE CHRISTIAN SCIENCE MONITOR. *Christmas In the Barn, Praise in December, Return Flight*

COLLEGE ENGLISH. *Wild Grapes*

COUNTRY JOURNAL. *Doing the Animals*

THE FARMINGTON VALLEY HERALD. *Christmas Bat, Flower Man*

THE HIRAM POETRY REVIEW. *Spring Song*

THE NATIONAL FORUM. *Jim's Garage*

THE LITERARY REVIEW. *Cat, Her Will, Invitation, Oscar* (as *Wood Man, Ice Man)*

LONG POND REVIEW. *Independence Day, Smith*

PEMBROKE MAGAZINE. *The Bats*

POEM. *A Country Death, In Wyeth, Tobacco Barn, Training the Wilderness*

POET LORE. *Doe*

POETRY VIEW. *Eight Feet Taller than a Worm*

PUCKERBRUSH REVIEW. *Getting Religion, Harry Noble*

THE SMALL POND MAGAZINE OF LITERATURE. *The Bishop Orders His Funeral, Flower Man, March 4, The Omen, Prayer*

THE TEXAS REVIEW. *Above Us* (as *Hawk*)

WIND LITERARY JOURNAL. *Carrie Wolf, In Conclusion, Salon, So Much Will Not Say No*

YANKEE. *And the Crippled Shall Dance, Christmas, Christmas Bat, The Child Who Took Forever, Ice Fire, Man with Geese, New England Greenhouse, Tree Man*

Contents

I

II

III

IV

I

Return Flight

High over the eastward rolling earth
I head for home. From here
all's one. The floes of ice increase
until the sea's the white of Gander
and Gander solid ice
which melts to the south, allows
the turned earth
this motley of black and brown,
these olive pastures speckled white
and pinkening hills. I agree.
I'm no less

new, no less prepared to understand
the peepers chiming in the bog,
the drunken wag of the new lamb's tail,
the blackbirds' squawk.

It's time we tried again,
my land and I.

Frog Day

The fen I live by is all a gabble, like ducks.
But it isn't ducks. Some other hosanna.
Verily the scum has begun to bulge, go bug eyed,
jump like Judgment Day.
And I am less defunct for this, more apt to sing,
feel my muse arising from the muck within.
Lo, look! Her peach of a throat is full
of spring, and she's begun to croak some code
it's up to me to crack.

The Burning Off

Abroad in morning fog I
coil, uncoil, disperse, assume
diversity of shape.

What's this—White Throats
on the wires,
half bird, half not. Hello
small counters. Maybe you're
hanging over billiards,
little tabs keeping score?

Let's see if I can stare you
down, adjust the tally
and there
I can,
my looks are palpable, a cue.

Thanks, birds. Fog's lifting
in me. The ghostgrey land
is green,
a sort of gaming table
and look

I'm less intangible than ever,
am full of me,
lungs filling, filling.

New England Greenhouse

Nothing doing here,
no goings on,
not a soft lipped orchid
or lily is loose.
Whatever is, is.
The sky is the sky—
whatever served for heaven
has fallen, is glass
the rats translate
to sand.
What was a green house
is a whistle for wind,
a scurry.
Where smooth gears moved
the heavens
with a sort of hum
is nothing now, nothing
but snow
curled in corners,
rust half through
with a boiler and coils,
and a sapling
up from the cellar
heading strictly
for the clear cut sky.

Independence Day

FOR NAOMI AND GERRY

Old Glory, and the drum major stepping high
as if Main Street burns his fancy feet like ours,
bare, so hot we stand them on their sides.
Next the trumpets aimed at the sky, the big bass drum
with the first of the thunder reserved for the 4th
and cymbals clapping, clapping.

Always the fire truck, bells on
and a clown aboard to spray us
with juju bees, red hots and root beer barrels.

At the fair
pink cotton spinning in a wind of its own,
the wheel of fortune chirping
and everyone about to win the biggest panda ever.
Dusk—and sparklers weaving, granting wishes
left and right,
the fair grounds going round and round.

Now let there be lights all over the gazebo, all over
the tubas pumping out Sousa
and last the works—a sky all boom and oom pah pah,
a sky more spangled than the Greenfield Band, a sky
still at it years after Old Glory fizzles,
is shreds of smoke.

Great Northern

Now the diesel-drone of De-limbers, Tree-harvesters,
the whole Great Northern Paper Company
going strong, forgetting the moral

I stumble upon, this engine
left half a century ago to wilderness
on rails now rusty earth
which once were bright from Eagle Lake to Umbazooksus
for flatcars piled with timber.

The boiler is rusted through,
a den for fox, fox stench the only heat
where once the stoke-door steamed.

The Great Northern Paper Company believes
in its De-limbers, Tree-harvesters. They are very large,
have long necks that lift and stretch
and noisily browse, forgetting
only the small
survive.

Tobacco Barn

Only the sun works this place, sneaks in
through half-shut slats that opened once
on sky enough
to cure the leaves,

tobacco leaves wide as sombreros.
The names of the Kilroys who were here
are fading from the beams they rode.
Nothing is going on

but light. That and the Bittersweet
burrowing in, insinuating up
and out, as once the tall tobacco broke
through clouds of net to celebrate

the sun; and a wind which knows
the ins and outs, the stops of the barn
by heart
and plays it perfectly. I kneel

to sift for history. In the dust
no longer at its dance
I smell the amber past.
Tobacco. The earth is steeped in it.

Jim's Garage

Sunset declares for Jim's Garage,
congratulates the cracks
in every pane

and turns the blues
(a cloud of exhaust, a bottle
of windshield solvent,
a pool of oil, and Jim himself
in coveralls for a front end job)
to gold.

Hung on the wall the hubcaps
(strange devices
Packard Hudson Studebaker)
shine.

For the moment five mechanics
pose, like history.

Doing The Animals

In the darkening barn
(old boneyard of birds and moles,
small rabbits)
to do the animals
I'm buzzed by a bat. I whistle

hello, I whoo an owl, in touch
with all that hangs from beams—
these coils of baling twine, a web
of tractor chains, the paw
of Nuggie the cat, old friends.

The barn's all eyes,
small eyes to watch for grain,
big eyes to watch the small eyes
watch. I get along
with them all.

In clover the ewes in rut
regard me as a possibility
and rub.
The ram stands off, eyes me.
I eye him back.

Ice Fire

FOR GLADYS EGDAHL

The winter I was twelve
the ice froze fast and clear.
We rushed to celebrate
before they came with saws and spikes
to harvest the lake to stack it
like bales of hay

and got there first.
With stumps and limbs from Tully's field
we built the biggest brushpile ever
and threw on top
my rocking horse, Anna Camke's dollhouse,
boxes full of building blocks
and Erik Tilton's logging truck
with the three wheels gone.

Some kerosene and up she went
so high the moon bounced about
at the top of the fire.
We cheered as the dollhouse caught,
skated circles around it.

When the whole thing collapsed
and our shadows were lost
in the dark beyond
we backed off, watched thick smoke
go flat in the wind, a sort of mane.
Next day they sawed.

II

In Wyeth

In Wyeth we never see
so see the more
the thunderheads
an old hound points as if
they are fair game

and do not see
so see too vividly
in pickaxe and shovel
red with clay
at rest against a rotting stump
the old dog's death.

In Wyeth we are not shown
the way a girl who shores herself
on arms like bone
has hauled herself from house
to barn, from barn to field.
We know.

The art is to suggest, not say
until we see
not exactly the old man's dory
scrubbed and caulked,
its bow line neatly coiled
in the bone dry loft of a barn—

not exactly that and not exactly
loss, or all that makes loss
gain, but something like
all three.

She Scatters His Ashes

FOR JOCIE

After so much dying
his ashes
come clean
do their dance
for her
scatter
shine
and settle on water
small fish

and she herself
belly-whopping
jack-knifing
lazing
like a water lily
slick
under water
his kind of fish.

Old Girl Running Circles Around Us

And just like that the sky is green,
breathing is a science,
our ears begin to sing. Abruptly
the poplars stop showing the whites
of their leaves
and for the moment we move no more
than time

then make for the bulkhead doors,
the cellar's far corner
and take our places, hands knotted
like roots.
We listen, listen, say little
then *Grandma's missing!*

When I find her in the yard
she's quiet as the coiling sky,
says it's time she went straight up
in the eye of the Lord,
smack into the midst of His mind

and gets away from me—
runs laughing around the house
as if she's warming up the wind.

Oscar

FOR OSCAR AND GLADYS EGDAHL

He was where stove-length maple,
birch, black locust
came from,

the reason
dawn crackled all winter
and potbellieds glowed
like Ida Reds, Rome Beauties.

You should have seen
his Belgians steam down
Grand Avenue. Their brasses
multiplied the sun.

And Lord how he cut up winter,
gaffed great chunks of it
to the icehouse, stacked it,
wrapped it in sawdust

he was that sure of summer.
And will not die himself
though dead these thirty years.
Memory's a shed for seasoning

the hardwood, heartwood
of him, the past an icehouse
full to the roof,
the place to pass dog days.

She

can fell the old red maple,
cut quickly from the top on down,
chain saw in one hand,
tree in the other—

can give the big rat snake
after eggs in the coop
a boot,
swing a hen around her head,
snap its neck—

can tackle the ram, sit him up
and fleece the beast
before he comes to.

Evenings she embroiders
dog-tooth, paintbrush, ragwort.
Her fingers
dart like hummingbirds.

The Flower Man

walks humped
as if his head's too heavy
for its stalk.

Truth is
he's bent above so much so long
he walks the way he works.

Banks his place with leaves
and winters like a root.
A blossoming of smoke is all.

And the smoke dies back and
he's made it
up before skunk cabbage

can uncoil, his tractor's mutter
better news
than any gaggle going north.

Man with Geese

Reasonable
this man stalking
the geese
feeding like wickets,
a few on duty
flapping him off.

Reasonable
a man in mud
above his boots
for the first geese
of the year.
A camera's his reason.

And why not clap
when they flap at him?
He wants a shot.

But this—
a man to his knees
in mud,
his camera still
in its case,
clapping and clapping
long after the geese
are up and away.

The Bishop Orders His Funeral

Please live it up when I go
and for a hearse something snappy—
a van with bells on to sell the kids
ice cream, popsicles.
I won't be where you think I am.

How can I say this?
Imagine a balloon with wicker cockpit.
Now you see it flat out,
a flop

and now with a hiss
it's blossoming all colors
rising in its element, going going
in morning mist
and shining through a break
before it's gone for good.

That's me.
Just when you think I'm nothing,
a stiff
I'll be a launching, a magic,
a cause for whistling and applause.

Eight Feet Taller Than a Worm

He was eight feet which
leaned akimbo back and roared over
things like the men on the moon.

He lasted two days
before his arms fell off,
his laugh went out with his
bad black teeth
and the sun in a rush unbuttoned him.

His carrot of a nose began to sag
around the sixty-fifth hour
after which it was all over:
body all but disappearing
last night,
head smashed to bits,
the same old story.

Now he's back where he began:
a snowball, stones and a carrot.
The snow will melt tomorrow
and some rabbit will eat the carrot
when we're not looking.

In spite of which he was
eight feet taller than a worm
and he had his laugh.
Let's hope they can say as much
for us
when we've gone underground.

Training the Wilderness

The mites and moles, the weeds may inherit her world
over her dead body, she says, still kicking
though the night is a woe of weeds sucking the soil,
mice clicking their teeth, hijacking seed, and cutworms
clipping away, small scissors.
Oh loud with larvae lacing leaves and galling trees
is the night, and always the grubs, undermining
beneath the blatant business of coons in the corn.
She cannot sleep for such a racket.

And if she does, her dreams are great with groundhogs
and hedgehogs, aphids, fungus gnats, mealybugs
and spidermites, thrips and mightily mandibled beetles
all doing to that perfect cauliflower, her brain
what they would to her formal gardens, her disciplined
hedges and dogwood, her triumphant victory garden. . .
except that they can't!

For she is up and at them with the sun, a bluebird
after worms. You can find her any day dropping beetles
one by one in kerosene like lobsters in a boil,
training shrubs in solid geometry, spraying her sky.
Her iris know her well enough to stay put in the part
of the plot she has granted them.

Come cocktail time she hides in the corn, waiting
for woodchucks. Just let one eye a Butternut
she's something,

arms and lungs enough to scare the living daylight
down *its* hole.

The bugs are busy evolving an answer to her energy
but for the time she has them properly
and whatever else would mess with her world.
One might wish that world more this way or more that
but never her, lest everything civilized cease.

Salon

Creation has learned its lesson here,
won't scratch for fleas or stalk or breed
where dehumidifiers hum like crystal spheres.
Though all that roar or howl are on display
they know their place,
politely gold or amethyst or jade.

The eagle won't stoop to destruction,
understands the lamb, takes his instructions
from above.
If the antelope bears a lion
it's the antelope's idea,
he will not bleed
and Satan sleeps coiled, content in his tree
with never a dream of a maiden sweet as fruit.

In Conclusion

FOR LIB

They do not like the looks
of death, try not to breathe
while changing what they take
to be me. It's not. I'm on

the mile or so of burning dust
I once walked daily for the mail.
I turn my bare feet on edge,
cool them in mud,
curl a double-jointed toe
around small stones, let fly
at trees

and vaguely in the big tin dipper
see tall sky, braids,
a crooked smile.
The water calms. I clarify.

Invitation

FOR E.A.M.

She keeps to herself this secret
of twigs and twine,
snake skin, horse hair, wasp paper
in forsythia trimmed like a hood
around the nest

from which, expecting, waxwings
sang all April
yellow, tawny, crested
songs. They were mistaken,
they left.

Dog Days. She trims to keep a gap
for waxwings in forsythia
and in herself another
for whoever she was when she was
at home in herself

and looked the part,
her skating costume polka dotted,
billowing, huge ruffles at the neck,
one leg in the air like a tail,
arms balancing, head cocked
to sing.

The Child Who Took Forever

I showed the proper pity for a child
who took forever,
who entertained wasps on her arms
dawdling, spoke a language
soft and meaningless as drool
or so I thought. My daughter said
listen slower.
Today I found the child
by Tilton's Creek,
hair sweeping the water,
talking with the thing
that if you wait like a weed
comes out of its hole in the bank
and points its ears at you.
Or so she said.
I listened slow. She knew
which foot had one claw missing,
which eye was brown, which black,
which move meant
Come with me.

And the Crippled Shall Dance

Her head, too large for her
wobbles
under the laying on of hands,

big hands accustomed to tools.
Her incoherent eyes
go still beneath a heaven of hands

and when they're free to move again
are perfect, dance together
as if they've practiced for years.

Getting Religion

Turned status quo myself I watch
the cove
do whatever coves do
and now this group of boys,
the newest in restlessness
felling trees
to build their kind of fire

whooping, wigwamming hemlocks,
spruce, old buoys, driftwood,
half a lobster pot
and topping it off
with a pair of jockey shorts
and Debbie's bra.
One side of the pile
is the rotted ladder from the pier.

What's that to them
who clown around
on the roof of the lobster shed,
dive thirty feet
to what may just be deep enough.
We'll see.

They must have made it
for there they are in dories
herding a school
which zips so fast from boat to boat
it's mostly hooked on mackerel trees
and flapping on the pier.
They hack, throw fish heads up

like skeet for low flying gulls
and leave the guts to crabs.

Now here's a sight. The boys are
quiet, hunker on rockweed
to watch the newest in restlessness
make mincemeat
of fish guts, crabs, and everything.
The eel is big around
as Johnny Thompson's forearm,
big enough to give a boy religion.

Carrie Wolf

Carrie Wolf was a disgrace, kept hogs
in her cellar
and chickens everywhere.

Summers she slept out back with a .22
the better to get a bead on the varmints
gnawing her pea patch, and children too.

One look at her, things grew.
It wasn't right. Come May, her chestnut
looked like Christmas—and we knew

why. Any day they'd hang her from it,
a witch who had it coming when we heaved
the worst we had at her on Halloween.

And what she did
when she caught us filching the biggest
luckiest nuts her chestnut grew—

what she did
was she gave us sacks and a helping hand
and

Carrie, that was real fine burlap
you saved for us.
You shouldn't have.

Bones

FOR DAVID RODGERS

It's bones with him, all bones.
Needs a wife to clean him up
the gal who runs the p.o. says

and out at his place
I agree, except about the wife.
Truly he's in bones. Wing bones
hung from the rafters

wheel like gulls
and chime. Horseshoe crabs
and horseshoe crabs are stacked
in a corner

and what those ribs
are doing in the sink, God knows.
Tide by tide, memento moris
multiply. His place has turned

so white
the lips, pearl pink, of a conch
seem obscene. It's nothing
to find in the dining room

a whale, its man-long skull
laid out on the table, its bones
all properly boxed
and tagged with labels reading

Hello, my name is ___________
What's yours? The blanks
are numbered 1 to 3,487.

Catechized, I know what I know—
my name is Bones. And yours?

A Country Death

Her heart has stopped banging about,
a jackhammer rattles her frozen plot

and here in her kitchen where no one
has lit a fire to warm his bones

a line of snow across the floor
is pointing from the door

to her geraniums
and by them, taking the sun

the rocker she'll be riding,
impatient with such civilizing

in the best room where they have her
where she never was at home.

Who else will see the fire's stoked,
the back door filled with oakum?

Her Will

It was her will that her remains be borne
out the kitchen door without the pomp of pine
and through the slant light, cathedral arch
of the barn grown sweet at milking time
past spires of onions
on to a congregation of clover.

It was her will that she be committed to
the meadow, to all that would polish her bones,
translate her flesh to loam so rich
the roots would utter her in ways
the sun would never forget,
the wind forever praise.

Smith

Outside, ice hung from the eaves.
The land was hard
as the ploughshares, pitchforks, spades
he forged

where so much heat made iron supple
as summer
and the old man's muscles
worked like water building over boulders
in the river he swam as a boy.

All winter, his last, he hammered
and bent,
his bellows breathing heavily.

As always the elements were winning.
Ploughshares, pitchforks, spades
were his response.

Harry Noble

spent the winter tying flies
so apt they must have made
a mayfly or a caddis
feel inadequate without a hook

and the season casting,
talking Browns and Rainbows
into what he'd made for them,

working each hook slowly, slowly
out, not ripping a thing,
jaws going like theirs

and throwing them back
or more properly
launching them in shallows—

launching all but the woebegone
who wore a sort of rusty fungus
the shape of hands.
(You never saw *him* touch a trout
dry handed.)

With those who worked the creek
most ably, the minks, the otters
and coons, he knew his place.
He'd spend good fishing time
on all fours in the mud

searching for a snarl of line
he'd dropped where one of them
might be the worse for it.
There were snares enough, he said,
without his own.

Tree Man

Jacob can have his ladder,
angels, the whole business.
Give me any day the man
with gaffs on his boots

who works his way straight up
a hundred feet of locust,
chain saw hanging behind
like a monkey's tail.

Give me the man
who hangs by a strap
in the middle of the sky,
stands on air

with the sun at his back,
does what he can
and drops down to earth
by a single strand.

Girl with Lilac in Her Hair at Twilight

Whether lilac does
this
for her to wear
a sprig
in hair not gold
not rose
not quite

or she is here
for purposes of
lavender
waiting
to be carried off
in a blaze of hair

or both
for a sky from indigo
to violet

admire
admire

III

Celebration

A dozen apples in December
shrink and wrinkle, go from dark
to darker, hang by threads
no thicker than our own.
And yet how like to ornaments
a dozen apples in December
and how the sparrows, reeling
wassail on the earth-gold wine
a dozen apples, aging, brew
beneath a low and southern sun.

Noeling in the Hoosegow

FOR GLADYS EGDAHL

The Christmas the church burned down
we did have an organ, and sister—
well, she pumped so hard
she pounded the town hall floor

right over the heads
of the drunks in the lock-up
below. She meant it, was fiercely
in favor of God

but not of how
when God Rest Ye Merry Gentlemen
ended, it didn't
in the underworld

accompanied by banging and jangling
of bars, slurring
into Away In A Manger off key
but softly

softly
until... she played along.
This time sister did her pumping
gently.

Being six
I said It was wise men. No one
said no.

Christmas in the Barn

I was nine and waiting
Christmas Eve
for the animals to kneel

and speak. Not to miss
a word, I was early, bearing
apples, carrots, turnips.

I gave my gifts,
I scratched the beasts,
I settled in the straw

and just at twelve
by the bells from town
the miracle was

I spoke Clydesdale,
I carried on in Lamb.

Christmas Bat

An hour till midnight service
and the sexton has fired up the furnace.
What a banging of pipes for Christmas.

Look, a bat abiding in the rafters
is flying low above the manger.
He tips his wings in praise

if only of a mite from the evergreen.
And something mute, inhuman kneels in me
awaiting the gift of song.

Back and forth in the nave
I hear the shuttle of wings like pages
turning to the proper carol.

Praise in December

Speak ye well of the meadow mice,
wee things to have weathered
the freeze
with breath enough to spare
to leave a rime like stars
above each burrow in the field.
Bring gifts, bow down, and learn.

Christmas

day is done. Wherever the trees
aren't violet on a field of white
they're white on deepening blue.

Carelessly a ribbon red as wrapping
lies along a line of hills.
The opening is done.

What's left to give
is simple as violet on a field
of white.

IV

The Inside Cat

Barn cats be damned.
She is the inside cat,
the one

who'll laze
around
and ha!

snatch the first line
of a poem. She mouths it,
title dangling,

drops, bats,
plays with it,
settles back

with one eye open, and
wham—has another.
By dawn she's nabbed enough

to come up
from the basement of my mind.
She gives it all to me.

Dawn on the Allagash

FOR BOB AND MARGY HOLDEN

Like dreams recalled
orb webs which faced the wind invisibly
and tossed all night
are visible at dawn by dint of dewdrops
strung concentrically.

Where creek meets river
the mist grows coherent,
a slate-blue heron, head cocked.

And always moose
the color of cedar
soft-shoeing the deep-piled moss,
racks snapping the brittle dead of ash and birch
come down to the water, snuffle Allagash,
heads wholly under
and up like waterfalls.
They chew, stare off somewhere I do not see, move slowly
upstream, rearranging the river.

Pheasant in the Cherry Tree

The plot thickens.
The cats fat on winter mole
asleep in the barn

a late sun gilding the glass
behind which I am
like something mounted
a curiosity
watching

what has been testing
with hoarse and rusty iambics
for cats
for me

come out of the woods
and start and stop
in bronze
tan spots
red mask
white collar

and start
walking maple shadows
on the snow
careful
careful now
like anyone skipping cracks
on a sidewalk

approaching choke cherry
as if it's no concern of his
as if no candy's hanging

looking anywhere
but at the lowest branch
checking left
right

making an awkward leap
splay-legged
like a boy with his eye
on an apple a little high

and pinching it
a bit of red
in his beak
and another and

at last highjumping
to the branch overhead
to settle down
to business
and abruptly

through for the day.
He is again
his own parade.

Sickle Moon: A Little Lunacy

Fact is the moon's the moon.
Fact is, however, not enough for us.
That's no new moon, you say

but a gypsy palm
with a crystal ball
which now you see and now you don't.

Nonsense, says Cat. She knows
it's a smile so ambitious
the face is fading fast

and Owl would have it a slice of eye,
a talon's worth
to see if the coast is clear.

So who am I to stick to facts?
Let's say the slice up there's a rind,
the rest a memory

of melon in the mind of melon.
Meanwhile the moon is sure it's moon
and earth's the metaphor.

Squirrel

FOR SIBLEY WATSON

I am the beast, I ride the snow, my fire
burns warm within. All you with fangs

ha ha! I get from here to there, I cope.
I shiver my tail for a start, and go

leaving all of my shadow behind—and stop.
I wait for the shadow I threw to catch on

then climb my tree so cleverly
I'm always on the side away from thee

O Death with thy claws and a grin.
I win.

Above Us

he circles, always
has been part of things,
was one of the beasts
of Bethlehem—dark star
riding wild the wind
while lambs and cattle
bowed below.

He circumscribes our ways,
cuts jaggedly
the sky,
is perfectly in love with us
as any creature knows,
its time come round
to thrill between
his darkening shadow
and him.

The Bats

FOR GERRY SHERTZER

I'll call them more than blind benighted hangers on,
say they set their bounds with deeds like so—
a flight from under the southwest eave
to Salter's oak,
then to the old sugar maple, two hundred feet
to the silo and back to the oak—deeds to the sky
I duly recorded, drawing a bead on the bats.

I did not know until
I'd emptied the sky, unwilling to share the house
with what would suck us dry and milk the cows
how like small hands
the claws at the peak of Beelzebub's wings,
how fine the down in von Richthofen's ears.

I dug their graves with care. I lowered more than
stricken tents of skin and bone.

Cat

My teacher's a calico cat. She deals directly—
tastes a spatter of blood left over from
two weeks' worth of kitten

with broken bones for a head, a mouthful of worms
to suckle, a crush of dirt for roof.
She researches
every nook where the curl of a kitten once was

then recalls the remains of a litter,
jumps a tail, piles on, calls them out to play.
She knows enough to leap, do flips in mid air,
play ball with the rest to celebrate their lives.

Doe

There's nothing will soften
the truth I've stumbled on.
Fact is

the neck's pulled back
the way the dogs would have it.
Tongue gone, ribs gnawed.

I know, I know
she feeds the grass,
the grass grows tall, all that.

I do not forgive.
White bone is what she is,
white bone

who once at dusk would leap
the grass, for a moment
gold.

The Birthing

Dark birthing shed, damp straw
and under it, half buried
this lamb all set to go,
mouth open which will not close.

And I—not here to get a grip
to pull him through.

I work the legs to make him rise
who is perfect in each respect
except this one.
If I breathe in him, if I
pound his heart—

the children,
they must not see, not him,
not me. This is the truth
we do without

so little a matter of flesh
and blood
the hide moves hard against
the bone. It is,
after all, just weight, a thing
I dangle arm's length from me,
the cord and afterbirth swinging,
swinging. I will not think

except I do
of her, pretty girl and bright

who gagged herself and had
her child

and tucked him in
a plastic bag,
the cord, cold tail
half out.

Like her, oh Christ like her
I'll hide dead weight,
I'll bury it deep, I—

hold this thing to me, hold
every part, my face in wool,
walk in
the living room
like that. Their eyes meet mine.
We will not be the same.

March 4

The winter is muted in mist,
the chill is off, signals on,
the barnyard geese are game.

But mostly the season is silent,
only a mutter of melting lake,
the goings on of creek.

Oh, and the cow got loose today
and threw the sky, all fours
stiff and off the ground.

That's all. No frogs, no pails
on tap, no coloring except,
except...

Magician

He bows, comes closer than seems safe,
washes his hands with air,
shakes out crisp white cuffs like snow,
bows again
and pulls an apple branch from thin air.

He touches it once, twice, thrice
and plays a few trills on it until
with the magic
we stood so long in the cold to see
it simply and suddenly blooms.

Next the fillers:
from his hat as nonchalant as March
coons, possums, one or two small bears,
some whistling swans—the usual.

For finale he vanishes into the smile
of a child who steps right up,
vanishes
like face cards up a sleeve.

Spring Song

When winter croaks, turns green
as frogs,
when tremendously we see the buds
to be the buds they've been
since fall
and hear the sap's obscenities,
when seeds begin to sing ho ho
and pop,
there's nothing in Ovid I'm not.

Prayer Upon Hearing the Salmon Have a Chance Against Ct.

Come dancing, come spanking upriver
O Salmo Salar, a fact after all
as much out of water as in it, in love
with a smell you can never forget.

May less be dead, may grizzlies
hear the news and show themselves,
their swipe as smart as ever,
their paws as full of fish.

May cougars prowl and God knows what
come out of hiding
in you and me.

Wild Grapes

Consider these grapes,
the real ones, not the fat ones full of sun
with misty skin like a mooning lover's eyes.
Claptrap. No, the ones I mean
grow honestly in the shade of the trees
they climb. They're small and dark
like eyes that fix on you in a narrow pass
and know you cold.

Indian Summer

The game is up, the trees are spent
but the crickets won't hear of it,
play summer perfectly.

Someone's late corn, shucked
still squeaks, a screen door bangs,
the distant thunder dreams
as usual. How much insists

on itself —
this honey bee drunk on pears
and you on me and I
on you.

Staying Put

The tree toads would say they're winning.
In every tree's a him, a her.
Her him herhim himher him her herhim
they hum. Things are, however,

not in favor of toads. The millweed's up
and out
and high above's a babbling
heading south.

Still the Toads Triumphant
won't budge for fall. They're family
and making more. *We are,* they sing
and we will be.

Storm System

What was black all day
is deeply blue.
Low above the marsh
a line of swans cuts through
a red sun.
I'll walk South Beach.

The wind is with me, the moon
beginning to be. I too,
I blink my light
at who knows who
is walking the beach tonight
and out at sea, benign
the storm responds in kind,
its reds and yellows muted.

The moon
sends rungs to my feet
I could climb.
I walk for miles,
star light, start bright—

and the wind picks up,
reverses. Bits of wrack

whip by, beach grass, eel grass
sting.
My steps fill up with sand.

Beyond me
one end of the system ignites
and passes it on
outlining precisely a range
of thunderheads,
teeth grinning,
a hundred miles of them
or more
and more each minute, closing.

Behind a rack of cloud the moon
is pale. Cold stone, its fires
out. And who's to say
the brightest star
has not long since become a gap
in heaven, an appetite for light?

My own does little good against
such darkening.

That Time

When mist walks the river at dawn
and swallows swirl
like snow—

when bees carouse from pear to pear,
when barn cats quicken
and streak to stalls at milking time—

when an old hound bays the frozen sky
all night like a distant freight
and each heart picks up speed—

when things increase, burn bright,
it's time,
it's time.

The Omen

At dawn today the moon
was thin, curved,
a talon of sorts.

Not yet December
and the sheeps' water
stiff all day.

Night falls, the stars
keep a sharp eye out,
the hooting begins.

And now the silence,
the long sweep
meant for one of us.

So Much Will Not Say No

Consider the leaves, white oak,
how they nest in the snow
where each has warmed the cold
like a hand.

Salute a widow on the loose
in the woods.
She makes a lively man
of snow. He's just her size.

See on the snow the mark
of sudden wings, too slow
for there the mouse print goes.
So much will not say no.

Rennie McQuilkin

RENNIE MCQUILKIN views the rural New England of these poems from a small farm in Simsbury , Connecticut, where he and his wife raise an assortment of livestock. "Sometimes it's pigs and horses; right now it's sheep and a big herd of frogs in the bog out back." When not working the farm, he composes his poems and teaches at Miss Porter's School, Farmington.

He began writing poetry while teaching at Phillips Academy in Andover, Massachusetts. Since 1978 his work has appeared in such publications as *The Atlantic Monthly, Yankee, The Southern Review, Poetry, The Christian Science Monitor, The Yale Review,* and *The New England Review & Breadloaf Quarterly*. In 1983 he published a chapbook entitled *An Astonishment and an Hissing*. He has won a number of prizes including the New England Poetry Club's Ruth Fox Award, and has recently received grants from both the National Endowment for the Arts and the Connecticut Commission on the Arts.

Rennie McQuilkin was born in 1936 and grew up in Rochester, New York "around the corner from Sarah Couch," to whom he was married in 1960. He holds degrees from Princeton and Columbia Universities, and spent a year at Harvard Law School, where he "concentrated on Thomas Mann rather than Torts and Contracts."

In the tradition of the bard, McQuilkin believes that "poetry is best appreciated when read aloud" and has given readings throughout the northeast. His aim is to help poetry earn a place in the hearts and minds of everyone, for "poetry belongs to us all, not just the scholars and critics."

SARAH COUCH MCQUILKIN, whose drawings admirably illustrate these poems, graduated with a degree in studio art and art history from Skidmore College. She has since studied at the Museum of Modern Art, the DeCordova Museum, the New Hampshire League of Arts and Crafts, and the Hartford Art School. She maintains her studio in a converted barn on the family farm in Simsbury.

This book is set in Garamond with titles
in Perpetua, and was produced in New Hampshire.
Composition by A&B Typesetters, Bow,
and Miller & Lord, Inc., Mont Vernon.
Printed at the Transcript Printing Co., Peterborough.
Paper provided by Monadnock Paper Mills, Bennington.
Bound at the New Hampshire Bindery, Concord.